EMPLOYMENTISM

ABDUSSABUR KIRKE

This essay is not subject to copyright.

Abdussabur Kirke asserts the moral right to be identified as its author.

Lifeboat Press

Contact: abdussabur.kirke@gmail.com

EMPLOYMENTISM

The act of working to earn money constitutes such a large proportion of the life of most men and many women that if the act is 'wrong', if it is unbalanced and unnatural, then people cannot be right, balanced or natural. One of the features of the age we live in is the enormous predominance of salaried employment as the primary arrangement of productive work. This is what is meant by 'employmentism': the idea, or rather – since it is usually not conscious – the default, programmed outlook that salaried employment should be the norm, as if it had always been thus, or, to add speculation to fiction, that it has evolved to be thus.

It is no accident that the abolition of slavery in the European Empires and America during the run-up to the Industrial Revolution opened out onto the rise of employmentism. It did not happen without protest, just as the rise of paper-as-money did not arise without protest, indeed derision, until gradually it prevailed, conquered, set in, and erased all history. There was once an intellectual discourse against "wage slavery". Its proponents imagined that a utopian world could exist in which all men were free. That will not be the contention here.

The arrival of salaried employment as the dominant work mode also coincided historically with the final dissolution of the guilds.

To be clear: we are not concerned with harking back to the past or trying to resurrect something bygone. Nevertheless we would like to assert that there are natural ways of doing things which harmonise with how human beings are structured and behave – and there are ways unnatural. The man who defecates publicly is considered unnatural – and conversely somebody who is obsessed with cleanliness is considered imbalanced. Those are basic human functions, but what of the more complex human activities – like work?

Employmentism

Let us examine what the contract of employment actually is. The employed man, during his working day, is not his own man. He does not own his time; he has entered into a contract under which that time is sold. His time may be free before and after work. However, the working day is designed to encompass the eight or nine hours a man can give over to profitable activity. Since he needs the daily remainder, and the weekend, to recuperate, eat, partake in family life and fulfil other biological needs like exercise, what is really left of his time are the scraps. In terms of the contract itself, the man is in one respect owned, since the money he receives is, when it comes down to it, not related to his productivity or output. He is getting paid even when he achieves nothing. That payment, therefore, can only be for his readiness, awaiting the orders of his employer. So if perhaps he is not owned in the full sense, then he is certainly rented out – and as every landlord knows, it can be hard to evict a stubborn tenant.

Conversely, from the employer's point of view, this contract is such that it excludes the worker from the bulk of the profits of production. Bonuses designed using the technique of psychology to maximise an employee's output are, if anything, a reinforcement of that convenient set-up.

Far from being the employee's equal, the employer is obliged to remain above the employee. Some degree of hierarchy may well be natural and necessary in any human organisation, but the proprietor/employee configuration is more than a mere hierarchical nuance. They live in different worlds. It is no use arguing that just because some people can climb up out of the pit, everyone can. Patently everyone cannot. In corporate terminology, employees are "human resources" – the Oxford definition of the word resource being "a stock or supply of materials or assets". The employee is in that sense stock, an asset.

Not that this kind of ownership is the same as slavery in the legal sense. The slave is owned property and that ownership may be enforced by outside law. The employee, on the other hand, is bound in by a much more indefinite, but in turn equally significant constellation of interior considerations, urges and fears. The slave can run away. The employee signed the contract. Most employees will admit their lack of freedom, voicing it somewhere between triviality and serious vexation. They are free in name while acting the opposite. They may hand in their notice – to move to a new position of employment. Different masters, same transaction.

Employmentism

Hence the Leftist outrage at capitalist corporations enslaving nations under the guise of "creating jobs", "bringing investment" and "boosting the economy" to release that trickle-down hoped for in the imagination of economists, unthought-of by the poor of the place, who to all intents and purposes seem damned as slave labourers. We would suggest that the Leftists are impotent and always will be, because they are still caught in the lie of the names. They still believe "jobs" is synonymous with freedom – if only the capitalists would treat those poor people more equitably!

The reality of being an employee may go on largely unnoticed by the subject for some time; even an entire lifetime. His life may also be lived at very different levels of comfort, from crushing poverty, as in the Third World, to relative affluence as in the wealth zones. The essential contract, however, is the same.

True, the contract is mutually consensual. That is what is so remarkable. People sign themselves up willingly. Indeed, a "good job" with a "decent salary" has become a shining ideal to be aspired to by young, up-and-coming individuals of talent, and it is precisely they who, as I will contend further on, need to remain free. Or, employment is considered a vehicle on which to ride to higher things, done "in the meantime" until something better comes up, or until one sets oneself up as a lone escapee. Or, the person is more honest and openly declares his preference for the "security" of a stable position, the outside world being too raw a place. He has embraced employmentism.

The sensational portrayal – in movies, documentaries, history and books – of slaves whipped in chains will remain a necessary part of what passes as modern popular culture for as long as employmentism remains, in order to suggest to mass-man that he is enjoying freedom.

Now this pseudo-slavery of employmentism is complete and victorious. It has entered man's inner fabric, wherein lie the names of things. The terms "slavery" and "salaried employment", which describe things so similar, have been torn apart, the one posited as the essence of evil while the other ensconces itself triumphantly, facilitating the enslavement of man en masse. This illusion has broken in on man's inner being, leaving him fractured to say: "I am free to be employed."

◊

Employmentism

The contract of salaried employment is difficult to reconcile with the free man, because the employee can scarcely respond spontaneously to what life places in front of him with a balanced consideration of how best to serve the moment. Furthermore a fixed salary, combined with preordained working hours stretching months or years ahead, punctuated by holidays and coupled (in the case of talent) with promises of increased rewards and access to loans – all that brings with it an inexorable psychological effect, which is that the subject begins to mathematise his own existence. All is seen in numbers, quantity and chronology. The fixed salary exacerbates man's dangerous tendency to numericise his life, by which inclination he descends into the realms of imagined monetary exigency. Spontaneous generosity is under direct attack. Genuine choice is under attack. Helping others is under attack. The human potential for greatness is under attack. But there is a still more serious effect. The salary is a veil to all but the most grateful of people. It is a veil to seeing the Provider in all that is received, a veil to the joyful gratitude that is itself a gift for which to be grateful, since the salary comes by the hand of the resented master, so the taste of bitterness creeps in.

It is hard for salaried employees to see the ebb and flow of wealth and the weather patterns of their inner response to such tides. The nature of the salary hinders them from witnessing the miracle of provision in every moment. They are in the dungeon, safely rationed, with at most a tiny window onto outside affairs.

It would be wrong to suggest that salaried employment ought to be abolished. That is not the point. There are circumstances in which it is appropriate. What is at issue is that there must be some men and women who want to be free. For them and by them, other models of work, participation and wealth must be restored as the normative way – restored, for they exist in our bones and cells, as does the sense of what is balanced and natural, encoded in what we might call 'Behaviour DNA'. While cellular DNA determines the physiological form, Behaviour DNA – which is by no means separate from the cellular – acknowledges that the human form is not just physical, it is a known set of behaviour patterns. Those patterns, in balance, are called Fitra.

Islam is Deen al-Fitra, which means the Transaction of Fitra. As Muslims we have the supreme advantage in these matters of being able to refer

Employmentism

them back to the archetypal Prophetic model. The accessibility of that model where all other primal models have disappeared or disintegrated is part of Allah's generosity to us and one of the proofs of Islam. Even the act of referring back to the Prophetic model is itself Fitra: it is man's Fitra in the dimension of time. People out of kilter with their nature refer to other times, past, present or even future, or to mere concepts borne of human ideas.

As long as man considers himself his own ultimate property, he will always submit to the option of renting himself out, or trample up to be the exploiter of other humans, squeezing the maximum out of their work. Even his peers. Even his betters. Especially them.

When man realises he is created, owned by and on loan from his Creator, to be returned to Him, he can begin to see this differently. He has realised he is himself borrowing his body and its faculties, the attributes of ability. The contract is: he must use them for the sake and the service of the Owner, and at the appropriate moment he must acknowledge and testify to their Ownership, their Origin, their Manufacture. He is a testifying slave of his Lord. He moves in the world as borrowed property among the totality of borrowed creation, and is its superior and master in as much as he knows and acknowledges his borrowed status. He worships the Giver, he is the slave of the Giver. In the world he is free.

◊

Every intelligent man and woman should know and consciously choose the transactions into which he or she is committed, the nature of those transactions, and what their implications are. There will always be employees just as there will always be slaves, and there will be noble and good employees and slaves, and noble and good employers and masters.

Furthermore, this is not a call to jump headlong off the ship of salaried employment into the ocean of the unknown. It is a call to reflect on which ship one is on, where it is going, and what wisdom dictates. Act now? Submit? Wait? Such decisions will hopefully not be taken in the dark night of aloneness. Jama'at is required, real community, the counsel and the reflection of others. Those things are what constitute the lifeboat. Every boat needs a captain, even a lifeboat. That is the Amir. Is land in sight? In other words, what is the envisaged alternative to employmentism? The art is to know when the moment is to move and to choose one's advisors.

Let there be no doubt though that a move must be made. The man and woman who want to free others, to abolish injustice, to see worship and gratitude established, must themselves be free.

The natural DNA of Behaviour is Fitra. The Blood of Behaviour is actions, and when healthy it is Futuwwa, nobility in action.

The healthy Body of Behaviour is Asabiyya. It is the bonding together of the slaves of Allah, free in this world, by their recognition of each other. There is no greater bond; it is above tribe and family and race. It is not an ideology, nor even a religion. It is unspoken yet it shines and illuminates the world when it appears. Only those of inveterate inner darkness and poison hate it, and others are drawn magnetically to it.

These are the patterns of Fitra, natural society, glowing, resplendent, generous. They are within each human as much as biological DNA is – indeed they are linked to the biological, something which in itself constitutes an important subject.

They can be corrupted, or they can remain intact. And they can be healed.

Fulfilling them outside of Islam is inconceivable, since they are the orientation of actions between people towards the Creator in the given moment. They require equity and honour, which will break down among people who do not know they are being observed inside of themselves.

◊

Allah, subhanahu wa ta'ala, says in His Book (Surat al-Baqara, 197):

لَيْسَ عَلَيْكُمْ جُنَاحٌ أَن تَبْتَغُواْ فَضْلًا مِّن رَّبِّكُمْ

There is nothing wrong in seeking bounty from your Lord.

And in Surat al-'Isra, 66:

رَّبُّكُمُ ٱلَّذِى يُزْجِى لَكُمُ ٱلْفُلْكَ فِى ٱلْبَحْرِ لِتَبْتَغُواْ مِن فَضْلِهِۦٓ إِنَّهُۥ كَانَ بِكُمْ رَحِيمًا

Your Lord is He Who propels
the ships on the sea for you
so that you may seek His bounty.
He is indeed Most Merciful to you.

And in Surat al-Jumu'a, 10:

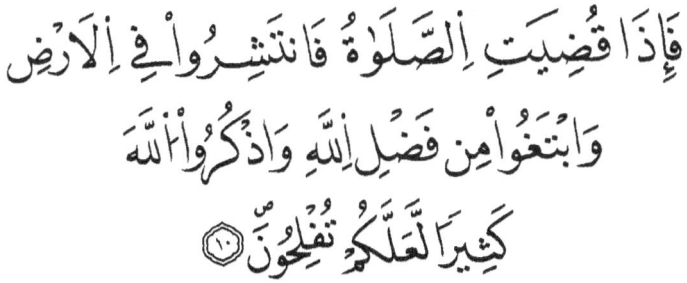

Then when the salat is finished
spread through the earth
and seek Allah's bounty
and remember Allah much
so that hopefully you will be successful.

Earning is described in terms of seeking the bounty of Allah, subhanahu wa ta'ala. This is the highest psychology of work.

◊

Employmentism

Trading describes the buying, moving and selling of goods, and has always been known to and esteemed by the Muslims. Its parameters are well documented, and the ways in which people tend to deviate in it are known. The Muslim trader who wishes good for others as well as himself would be advised to look first at contracts of partnership, in preference to salarying someone to do the work of selling, or in preference to borrowing from usurious institutions. Again, abolishing salaried employment is not the issue. The question is this: is it not possible that some of this bounty, since it is from Allah, can be shared, and indeed, might it benefit me to join in partnership with others in obtaining it? Employing salaried workers, even if it proves necessary, is a completely different and lower category of transaction and should be treated as such.

As for work such as manufacturing, engineering and the trades: if we can put aside the historical connotations and recover the essential structure; if Muslims can decide to work together without enslaving one another in salaried arrangements; if skilled persons of like profession can join together for mutual benefit – then what we will arrive at is the form of the Guild.

Employmentism

The Guild is, at its core, based around two dynamics. Firstly, that of skilled persons joining together in work and dividing up the proceeds in whatever way may be equitable – and equity of transaction is the subject of the Fiqh. Secondly, the relationship between the master and the apprentice – in other words, someone skilled and someone without the skill. Someone who knows and someone who does not know. They are not the same and they are not equal, but this is where the acquisition of skill and knowledge lies, and where man's potential for great learning finds a home. Even within the framework of post-Guild professional education, true learning still happens by transmission from the knowers. Everybody remembers their greatest teachers.

◊

It is up to leading Muslims in this age to restore these dynamics in the arena of work and trade, looking to the Fiqh as the map of the land. As such there are not two entirely distinct classes of "businessmen" and "'ulema", because people engaged in something must have at least the bare minimum of knowledge to know what is right and wrong, just as the man who prays must know enough Fiqh to pray. Among any grouping there are those who know more, and those who do not know, and the latter need to be protected by the former. People who know the Fiqh have a responsibility, but they are not a class apart.

The tide may appear to be against the establishment of such Fitri models. The enormous structures set up in modern industry and commerce, all now based on patterns alien to Islam, can seem self-protecting and self-perpetuating within their own implacable logic. Yet what is really more extraordinary is the dysjunction between their apparent strength and actual fragility. Allah says in Surat al-'Ankabut, 41:

$$\text{مَثَلُ ٱلَّذِينَ ٱتَّخَذُوا۟ مِن دُونِ ٱللَّهِ أَوْلِيَآءَ كَمَثَلِ ٱلْعَنكَبُوتِ ٱتَّخَذَتْ بَيْتًا ۖ وَإِنَّ أَوْهَنَ ٱلْبُيُوتِ لَبَيْتُ ٱلْعَنكَبُوتِ ۖ لَوْ كَانُوا۟ يَعْلَمُونَ ۝}$$

The metaphor of those
who take protectors besides Allah
is that of a spider which builds itself a house;
but no house is flimsier than a spider's house,
if they only knew.

Re-establishing Fitri models is itself work, and the difficulties encountered must not be interpreted too hastily as failure. The landscape of inequity in which we intend to build can make straightness seem almost bent, but there is nothing that cannot be put right with patience and good company, if Allah wills. With every difficulty, Allah has provided ease.

◊

That is the realm of work. By extension it has to be said that the Leader of people who wishes for good cannot be salaried and cannot salary his Close Circle. He must be what the Germans call *souverän* – a master, free, sovereign – and he must choose souverän men as his Close Circle. They together must be a refuge of the knowledge of Divine security, a zone of Asabiyya in wealth or poverty, and able to act. What is at the centre determines what the nascient body politic will become.

The Leader is the best of his people and the servant of his people, and his Close Circle surround him because they recognise the way things are, and they desire to spend some of the wealth of their selves in that high cause. Insert a salary, that contract belonging to the low status of chainless bondage, and the whole thing goes to ruin.

The Leader tried in vain to call on men from the ranks of the world's employees. They were not free to help, so in frustration he turned to that same device to tie down some men of his own. He built a salaried army but they were prone to desertion.

Do they sit with him because they are being paid to do so? When their hours are done, do they get up and leave? Treated as resources, will they not act out that dead role? When the time comes for them to point out the difficult truth against the tide of opinion or the Leader's pleasure, are they to fear for their provision? Or maybe, tired of pretence, they will dissent acrimoniously to break the bonds they have come to resent. The employer-employee dynamic does not befit the leading circle.

For the employee in business, the contract is a veil to the Provider. For the employee in the leading of men – which is politics – it is a veil to Allah as the One who bestows power and authority. Political employees might never fully understand. They see their authority as the gift of the employer and are prone to blindness. Blind to the sublime workings that bind men together in leadership when those men recognise that their inner predispositions and outer destinies are inescapable, and that only when they join, led by the man who should lead, will that destiny reach its full splendour. A man's authority is by legitimacy, and obedience to legitimacy ennobles the one who obeys.

The Close Circle of Leadership is based on legitimacy and runs on generosity, open and hidden, and concern for others, so that they deserve to be looked up to by the wider community, and their people love them and love their Leader. They may trade, they may earn, and they certainly may be wealthy, even if sometimes they are poor. But it is not for wealth that they exist: rather, it serves their purpose.

For the Leader and his Close Circle, their secret among themselves, unvoiced except on the tongue of the moment, is that for all the blessings they enjoy, they did not themselves acquire any of it.

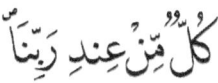

"All of it is from our Lord."
(Qur'an 3:7).

www.ingramcontent.com/pod-product-compliance
Lightning Source LLC
Chambersburg PA
CBHW022023290426
44109CB00015B/1289